Reading Wc
Everyday W

LEVEL 4

Mimi changes her mind

Nola Turkington
Series Editor – Jean Conteh

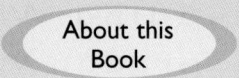

To the Teacher or Parent

This book is about a young girl called Mimi, who has to move with her mother from the city to live in the country. At first, Mimi is unhappy and does not like the country, but gradually she learns to appreciate the things she finds there. She performs a brave act that helps the other children to accept her, and she starts to become 'a country girl'. The subject of the story will be of interest to both boys and girls.

The book is designed for children to read on their own. The simple language will make it fun and easy for them to read. The pictures will help them understand the words.

Use the book like this:

- First of all, ask the children to read the title, look at the picture on the cover and tell you what the story will be about.

- Talk about differences between the city and the country. Ask the children which they prefer, and why.

- Let the children read the book by themselves. When they finish, ask if they enjoyed it.

- Let the children look at pages 28–32, where there are some questions and activities to help them understand and enjoy the story better.

Above all, let the children enjoy reading the book. This will help make them interested in reading. They will want to learn to read for themselves, and become independent readers.

'I don't want mud on my white shoes,' Mimi moaned.

She skipped round a puddle in the road. After rain, there were always a lot of puddles on the road.

'Take off your shoes, then,' Zoleka laughed.

Zoleka was Mimi's new neighbour. She ran ahead of Mimi.

Mimi felt very sad.
'I hate the country. I want to go back to the city,' she said to herself.
Mimi used to live in a big city with her mother and father. Father was a traffic policeman.

One day, there was a traffic accident in the city. Mimi's father died in the accident. Mimi and Mother were very sad.

Then, Mimi's uncle invited them to live with him in the country. Uncle was Mother's brother. He was very kind to them. But Mimi missed Father. And she missed the city.

Zoleka lived next door to Mimi. She took Mimi to school. On their way to school, they met a herd of cattle. The big beasts stared at Mimi. She shivered.

'Zoleka! Zoleka!' Mimi screamed.

There was a boy with the cattle.

'Hock! Hock!' he shouted to the cattle.

It was Sam. Sam was Zoleka's brother. Every morning, Sam looked after his father's cows. He went to school in the afternoon.

Mimi watched the cattle walk along the muddy road. Her eyes were wide with fright. She had never seen cattle up close before.

Mimi was late for school. She crept to her desk. Teacher scolded her new pupil from the city.
'Don't be late again, Mimi Mamela,' she said.

Mimi felt miserable. She missed Mrs Nkosi, her teacher in the city. She missed Lena, her best friend. Most of all, Mimi missed her father.

After school, Mimi walked home. Suddenly, she spotted a large brown and black snake gliding along the path. She was too scared even to scream. She ran! Mimi forgot about the mud on her white shoes. She ran straight through six big puddles!

No one was at home. Mother was weeding on the farm. Uncle was mending the hen house fence. Mimi raced into the house.

There were five fat hens on top of the table, pecking for food. They went wild. They squawked and flapped their wings. They flew round and round the room like a small tornado.

'Shi!' the city child cried. 'I can't believe it! Five big birds flying round inside the house!'

Next morning, very early, Uncle's red rooster woke Mimi.

'Cock-a-doodle-doo!' he crowed under her bedroom window.

'I wish I could hear traffic hooting, instead of that rooster. Then I'd know I was back in the city,' Mimi declared.

After breakfast, Mimi helped Mother to hang out the wet washing.

'Mother, when can we go home? Everything's scary round here,' she asked.

Just then, Uncle's big black dog ran into the yard. Mimi dashed through the gate. She raced towards Uncle's orange trees.

'Mimi Mamela, come back. Boxer won't bite you. He's only saying hello,' Mother shouted. But Mimi just ran faster.

It was quiet and peaceful under the trees. There was a beautiful smell of ripe fruit. It made Mimi feel hungry. She picked an orange. The juice tasted so sweet. She picked another orange.

Mimi walked between the trees. She came to an open space.

Suddenly, she saw something frightening!

Cows! Mimi wanted to turn and run. She heard a voice. It was Sam.

'Hello Mimi,' he said. 'The cows won't hurt you.'

Mimi still looked scared. Yesterday was the first time she had been near cows. Sam whistled through his teeth. At once, the cows lifted their heads.

'Ninzi, Ninzi,' Sam called quietly. A brown and white cow trotted towards him.

Mimi watched Sam milk Ninzi. When the bucket was full, Sam dipped a tin mug into the bucket and shared the warm milk with Mimi. She sipped slowly from the mug.

'I didn't know that you got milk from cows like that,' said Mimi. She licked the white froth from her lips.

Then they heard Mother calling, 'Mimi, Mimi!'

'See you, Sam,' said Mimi.

On Monday, it was raining again. The puddles in the road grew bigger and bigger. They grew muddier and muddier. Zoleka splashed past Mimi in the middle of the road.

'I love mud between my toes,' shouted Zoleka. 'You're a silly city kid. You're scared of mud! You're scared of cows! You're scared of chickens!'

Mimi sighed and tried not to cry.

'News travels fast in the country,' she said to herself.

Then the accident happened. The rain made the road slippery. Zoleka slipped and fell. She hit her head hard on a stone at the side of the road. Mimi rushed to help her. Zoleka lay still in the muddy road.

Mimi bent over Zoleka. She lay very still in the muddy road.

'Please, please, wake up,' said Mimi.

Desperately, she tried to drag Zoleka to the side of the road. Zoleka was bigger and heavier than Mimi, and she lay there like a log.

Zoleka did not move. She lay in the road.

Then, in the distance, speeding through the rain, Mimi heard the sound of a car coming along the road. She felt very frightened.

'If I don't stop the car, it will drive right over Zoleka,' thought Mimi.

In a flash, Mimi remembered how her father used to direct traffic in the city. She stood in front of Zoleka. She held her hand up, just like her father used to do.

'STOP! STOP!' yelled Mimi.
Just in time, the car driver spotted the small girl in the road. With a screech of the brakes, he stopped the car just in front of Mimi.

The driver jumped out of his car. Behind Mimi, he saw Zoleka lying in the road.

He gently picked up Zoleka in his arms. He laid her on the back seat of his car.

'Climb in,' he said to Mimi. 'We'll take your friend to the clinic in the village.'

The driver and Mimi waited outside the clinic while Sister Lebu examined the patient. Soon, she gave them some good news.

'Zoleka is awake now,' she said, 'but she has a big bump on her forehead and a bad headache. I've given her some medicine. In a few days, she can go back to school.'

'I'll take her home, then I'll take Mimi to school,' said the driver.

On the way to her house in the taxi, Zoleka held Mimi's hand.

'Sister Lebu told me you stopped the car,' she said. 'You're the bravest person I know. I'm very sorry that I called you silly.'

Mimi felt happy for the first time since her father died.

The taxi driver drove to Zoleka's house. Then he took Mimi to school. They met Sam and the cattle on the road. They waited for the cattle to cross the road. Sam ran to talk to Mimi.

'I heard about you acting like a traffic policeman,' he said. 'You saved my sister's life! You're very brave. Every morning for a week, I'll bring you a bucket of Ninzi's milk.'

Mimi laughed. 'Can I milk Ninzi?' she asked.

When Zoleka was better, she and Mimi became friends. Every day, they went to see Sam and the cattle. Mimi learned how to milk Ninzi.

'Shi, Mimi! You've become a country girl,' said Sam.

Mimi felt happy. She knew she would never forget her life with Father and Mother in the city, but now she liked the country as well.

Activity page

1. Look on pages 6 and 7. Think of three words that describe the cows.

   There are some photos of cattle on page 32. Which one makes you think of a *beast*?

2. Write down four things that Mimi did not like about the country.

3. The title of the story is *Mimi changes her mind*. What did Mimi change her mind about? What happened to make her change her mind?

4. Do you live in the country or a city? Write down four things you **like** about where you live and four things you **do not like**.

5. When you have written your list, compare it with lists written by other pupils in your class who have read *Mimi changes her mind*.

Activity page

6   Look on page 16. Why did Zoleka call Mimi 'silly'? How do you think this made Mimi feel?

7   Has anyone ever called you names? Write a short story about a time when you were called names.

8   Zoleka called Mimi 'silly', but she did something very silly herself. What was it? Why was it a silly thing to do?

9   What did Sam do to make Mimi feel less frightened about the cattle?

10 Have you ever helped someone to feel less frightened? What did you do? Write a few sentences about it.

Activity page

11 Think of three things children should do to be safe on the road. Make some posters to teach your classmates about road safety.

Here are some examples of road safety posters:

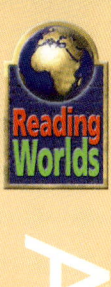

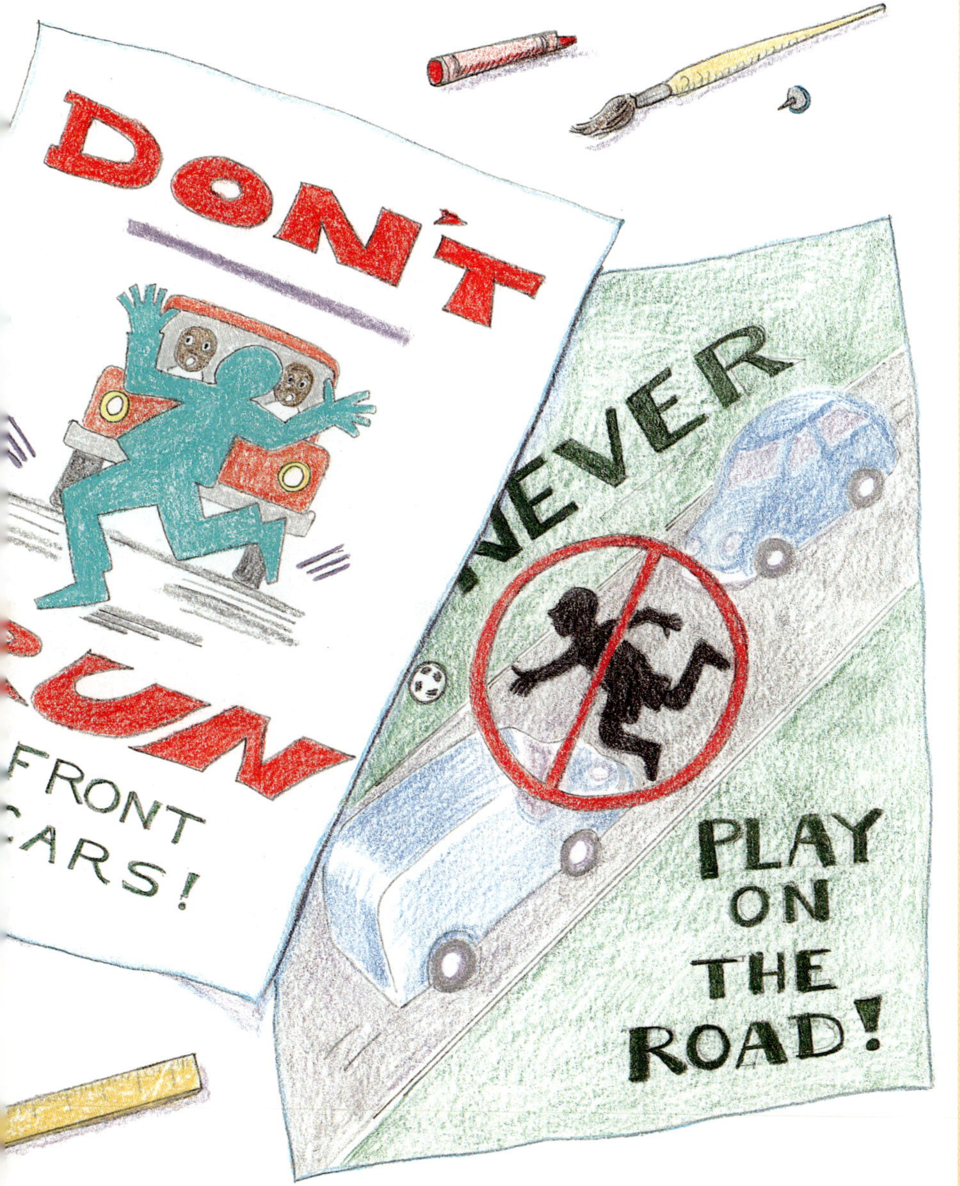
DON'T
FRONT
NEVER
PLAY ON THE ROAD!

Activity page

12 Here are some photographs of cows.

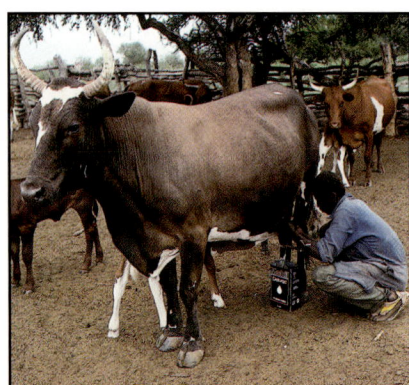

Cows in Botswana.

Cows in Kenya.

Cows in Botswana.

Cows in Uganda.

Have you seen cows like these? Which ones are similar to cows in your home area?

13 See if you can find out what other things cows give us, besides milk.

Don't go near bulls!
They can be very dangerous!